Y0-BRP-897

THE
CHRISTIAN
HOME

THE
CHRISTIAN
HOME

by
Ralph Heynen

Contemporary Discussion Series

BAKER BOOK HOUSE
Grand Rapids, Michigan

Copyright 1975 by
Baker Book House Company
Second Printing, October 1975

ISBN: 0-8010-4109-0

Printed in the United States of America

INTRODUCTION

To develop a healthy Christian home life in this time of many social pressures requires effort on our part. It does not just happen by itself. It is well to look at this as a challenge, rather than a matter of solving "problems."

Group discussion among Christian people is one of the finest helps in achieving a good marriage and family. Each person, every couple has something positive to give to others. Mutual sharing can be a powerful source of encouragement and can help to face the common concerns of everyday living.

Each lesson in this manual offers input material, Scriptural references, and discussion questions to give some guidelines for the discussion. The basic material was first published in *Bible Studies*, an adult paper, published by the Christian Reformed Board of Publications, the Education Department. We have edited each lesson considerably, given a Scriptural basis, and amplified and changed the discussion questions. We are grateful to the Publications Board for allowing us to use this material in book form.

The favorable response to our previous guidelines for discussion, *Creative Questions on Christian Living* (1967) and *Where Are You Growing* (1972) has encouraged us to present this manual on marriage and the family. We have repeatedly received requests for discussion materials on this subject.

We suggest that you read the input materials in your group session. Also read together the Bible passages that speak to the subject and see how they relate to the lesson, for they are intended to stimulate discussion by the members of the class. You will notice that a simple Yes or No answer does not satisfy, nor should this be a question and answer session. Choose the questions that are of the greatest interest to the group.

Avoid using trite and obvious observations. Try to gain fresh insights. The success of a discussion group depends on the number of persons who become involved. Not all questions need a definitive answer, for it is good that couples have unresolved questions that stimulate further meaningful communication at home.

This manual is offered with the hope and prayer that it will help to build a better Christian marriage and stimulate spiritual and emotional maturity in family living today.

I am deeply indebted to Ida, who has shared marriage and family living with me for over forty years. Her inspiration, her gentle criticism, and capable assistance in preparing this manual have made it a meaningful experience for both of us.

Ralph Heynen

CONTENTS

1

A HOUSE — OR A HOME?

"The Smiths have such a lovely home on such a beautiful street" is a comment often made by people in this superficial age. Actually, the Smiths may have a lovely house, but a pathetic home. Edward Guest tells us that it takes a "heap of living to make a house a home." We think of the home as a place for family living, but a house is a place where the family lives.

The modern family dwelling is a marvel of convenient living. Houses have been lighted, heated, and gadgeted in a way that our parents never dreamed of. We no longer struggle with clinkers, but just set a thermostat. We push a few buttons for the family laundry, another few buttons for the dryer, and it does a better job than Mother could do in her old-fashioned laundry and in half the time. We have refrigerators, frozen foods, ready-mixed cakes, and automatic ovens that make the work much easier. Some houses are showpieces, finely furnished and carpeted, with four or five bathrooms and convenient recreation rooms on the lower levels.

Broken Homes

But while all these fine split-level houses are going up in the suburbs, the number of families that are divided by divorce, or by a cold war, is constantly increasing. Many pastors spend a good share of their time trying to keep couples in a reasonable state of compatibility, to keep the family together in one way or another. For many people the home has become a house, a dormitory where people eat and sleep, and for the rest there is little that makes it worthy of the title *home*.

What is it, then, that makes a house a home? There are many answers for this, for we all draw our conclusions from our own parental homes, at least if this was a good and comfortable place in which to live out the early years of our life. But there are certain basic requirements that every home must meet.

The warmth of a hearth with a glowing fire is not enough to make a home, although it can help. A home needs the warmth of loving companionship and understanding. It's a place where you feel wanted and loved, and where you show this love again to other members of the family. It's the warm emotional atmosphere that makes a house a home. We must watch the emotional tone of the home. Is there a lot of bickering and quarreling? Is there too much shouting and threatening? Is there a lot of anger and hostility? These qualities can spoil the atmosphere of the home.

Increased Tensions

We face a world with many tensions. The salesman in a department store, the mechanic in a garage, the worker in a factory, or the bookkeeper in his office, all are subject to many tensions. Tensions of this sort cannot be expressed while we are at our place of business. When such a person comes to his home, he needs a place where he can feel at ease, where the pressures are not as great. But when he enters his house and finds that the same tensions are present there, he does not find a real home atmosphere. The home should be a place where the family can live in a relaxed way.

This does not mean that the home is an undisciplined place. A child gains his security when he knows just where the lines of behavior have been drawn. He must not only know what he shouldn't do, but also what he must do. He must take his place on the family team, to help to make that house a home. Too many dos and don'ts tend to make the home seem like an institution. Parents must not become policemen, or policewomen, to enforce the rules, but they must guide the young to learn the art of living. Of course, parents also need discipline. It is to be hoped that they have self-discipline to guide their own lives.

Parental Concerns

Parental guidance is needed, and if parents are to assume responsibility for the growth and development of their children, they must set goals and help the children to reach for them. Without this kind of direction, a child will feel insecure; he will have good reason to question whether his parents really do care for him and love him. No child can find his own direction when he is still young. The immature child is asking for guidance from a loving and hopefully mature parent. If he does not get it, he will feel lost and neglected.

When many parents see their children become little individuals who think for themselves, they think of them as "cute" or precocious. But if this streak of individualism is not properly directed, parents may find that in time they have an unmanageable child on their hands—a promiscuous teen-ager. We meet many people who try to give direction to the child when his patterns of living have already been set; the child will generally refuse to be directed at this late hour. Direction is needed early in life when the patterns of living are developing.

Where People Feel at Ease

I feel that home is a place where the members of

11

the family can feel at ease. I see some houses that have beautiful furniture, off-white rugs on the floor, and many dainty and expensive gadgets. I often wonder how the children can feel at home in such a setting. This is also true in the houses where the mothers have become housekeepers, with a compulsion to keep everything spic and span, and free from dust. There must be a place for a growing family of youngsters. If the house becomes more important than the people who live in it, it's not a home.

I believe that you can tell whether or not your house is a home when you listen to the family as they gather around the dinner table. What is the general spirit of the family? Does this become a time when parents must set the children straight, rebuking or punishing them? Is this a time for bickering and conflicts? Does the family use this time to gossip about the neighbors, or the in-laws? Does it happen rather often that one of the family members leaves the table in tears, unable to eat? Potatoes and meat do not mix well with arguments. The dessert loses its sweetness when there is a bitter attitude in the family. The home and family should be a place where people can laugh and have fun.

Influence of Children

Often a house does not really become a home until there are children. A few lively youngsters can do much to transform the spirit of the family. For some people a house does not become a home until the family has wept together. When some dark cloud of illness or sorrow has passed over the home, the family is knit together as never before. For when we rise again from the moments of grief we can see anew the joys and the sunshine of living together.

It's a wonderful thing when a family also prays together, for this helps to make a house a home. I do not mean just the routine prayers we recite at mealtime. But the fervent prayers that are pressed out of our hearts when we feel that we cannot face the battles of life alone, and our hearts cry out to God for His sustaining grace and love.

It's too bad that many fine houses have never really become homes for people living in them. We often say, "Home is where the heart is." But in too many homes there is not enough heart. There is toil, there is strife, there is pain, there are arguments, but the real ingredient is missing—a warm and sincere spirit of love.

Praying Together

To show our children the Christian influence in our lives requires that we give them some of our time. We have no right to be so busy with other things that we lose sight of the highest priority of life—to take the time to train our children in the Christian way of living and the Christian's use of his time. Many people develop a busyness complex, because they fail to heed the words of Paul to "redeem the time." We must seek to do our best for the great Giver of time, and be able to say, "Time, thou art not my master, but my Master and thine lives in eternity."

WHAT THE BIBLE TEACHES:

Proverbs 31:10, 12, 26-31 Describes the role of an efficient wife and mother. (Does this fit the modern homemaker?)

I Peter 3:7 Describes what a husband should do.

Colossians 3:19, 21 Describes the role of the father in the family.

EXPLORING OUR FEELINGS

1. How would you describe your parental home? Was it a happy place? How would you have liked to see it

changed? How does it influence your home and family today?

2. There is a lot of status-seeking in suburban living today. If you could afford it, would you like to have an expensive home with a pool and all the other luxuries? How would this affect your family living? Would your family be more happy there?

3. Excessive cleanliness in housekeeping can spoil family living. How do you know when the mother is excessively clean? Is it better that a home have that "lived in" look? Often a husband is dissatisfied with his wife's housekeeping. Does this mean that husbands can also be obsessively clean?

4. Several statements are made today about the home:
"The family that laughs together, stays together."
"The family that plays together, stays together."
"The family that prays together, stays together."
Which of these three is the most neglected in your family? Which of the three is the most important?

5. How can you tell when you are too strict, or too permissive in the discipline in the family? Is there a kind of discipline that keeps a house from becoming a home?

6. A man had a special room in his basement, decorated with religious art, for his daily time of devotions and prayer. How do you feel about this?

7. If you had to make a choice in your house, would you make a recreation room for the family, or a workroom or darkroom for your own hobbies? Your answer will reveal a good deal about your feelings about your family, and about yourself.

8. What can be done to create a better emotional tone in the home?

2

NO 50-50 MARRIAGES

Often, when couples come in for premarital counseling, they will say that they plan to have a 50-50 arrangement. Each partner will share with the other so that each carries 50 percent of the load. This is a beautiful statement, but it is not an ideal for a good marriage. The intentions are good. If the regular dinner hour is to be six o'clock, it will mean that the husband is home on time, and that his wife will have the meal ready at the proper time. They agree to show respect and love for the parents on both sides, and do it wholeheartedly.

It is ideal to have teamwork, and most modern couples feel that this is what they want. The husband is not expected to be a tyrant who can demand what he wants with the idea that his wife will obey him. The wife is to be submissive to her husband, but she should not lose her personality and initiative. She must not become a silent partner in the marriage union. Today the woman is quite aware of her independence, her abilities, and the contributions she can make. She does not lay aside these qualities in today's family, but she is willing to share her part of the responsibility in running the home.

Not Do as We Please

No husband is free to do as he pleases, nor should his mate feel that she has that right. There must be a sharing with each other; in an ideal marriage each partner recognizes the strengths as well as the weaknesses of the other partner. This kind of marriage requires mutual respect and love. It will take some time in marriage to learn how to work out the details of this teamwork, but as time moves on husbands and wives learn to know each other better and, hopefully, to love each other more deeply with each passing experience.

But this does not mean that there is a 50-50 type of arrangement, but rather that each partner has his role to play. Neither partner should interfere in the role of the other. Two people in marriage are to become one flesh; there must be a unity of purpose, a mutual agreement, and a common devotion to the life of the family. This requires that each shall give 100 percent of his effort and energies to the establishment and maintenance of the home.

A Power Struggle

In too many homes, there is a power struggle going on between husband and wife. This grows out of a 50-50 arrangement. No family or home can be divided equally into two areas, unless the partners agree to live in different parts of the house. There must be a total commitment to the family on the part of each.

If there is less than that, something is missing. There are marriages in which partners are not fully committed to each other and to their marriage. A girl of sixteen became pregnant while in her junior year of high school. The parents and the pastor pressured this couple to marry. After all, the child should carry the name of his father. However, the young man was neither ready for marriage, nor that much in love with the girl. But due to the shame of the situation the marriage was performed. The girl was too young to know what a real sense of commitment was, and the young man was rather halfhearted about it. Four years and two children later, the marriage broke up.

Basis for Marriage

The couple who has built their marriage on a

romantic sort of love or on physical attraction, will find that they must face hard realities when the honeymoon is over. It is not always easy for two people to live together. If there is no real personal commitment to the ideals of a Christian marriage, it is easy to let the marriage develop into a cold war. Differences become greater and greater, for there is no real desire to find solutions to problems.

I recently came in contact with a family that had suffered many reverses. There were some deep financial problems; the mother had been ill a great deal of the time; one of the children was suffering with physical problems. In such a situation nothing less than a deep personal commitment to the family can keep it going. It is not easy, and there will be times when the relationship suffers, but if there is a basic strong commitment, the marriage can weather the storms.

In marriage counseling it is customary to ask each of the partners whether they really want to make their marriage work. When one or both of the parties involved is not sure about this, it is a waste of time to try to keep them together by counseling. There must be a desire to work out differences and to make adjustments.

Looking over the Fence

Another type of marriage in which there is only a 50 percent commitment is one in which either the husband or the wife is looking over the fence at other mates. I find in recent years that this is far more common than many people suppose. Many of these "affairs" are kept as deep dark secrets, but they eat away at the very foundation of the family. For when one, or both of the partners does not have a deep sense of loyalty to the marriage and to his mate, the marriage will not be a good one. Affairs are one of the most destructive things in the family today. You would be surprised to know how often this is happening, even within the Christian community.

100 Percent Commitment

The love of which Paul speaks in Ephesians 5 is compared to the love which Christ has for His church. His is a self-giving love, not a selfish love. His is a love that gives 100 percent, not just 50 percent. It is a love that does not seek His own advantage, but is given wholly for His own. None of us reaches that ideal; but we should be working toward it. Each difficult experience, each joyful moment, and each prosperous adventure should lead us to a deeper sense of that kind of love.

The advantage of a love that reaches toward those heights is that it is not dependent on the health, the behavior, or the attractiveness of the mates. It is given wholly as unto the Lord. I recently met a mother whose husband had been unfaithful to her; but she said, "I still love him, and I can forgive him from the heart." We need more of that kind of commitment to today's family.

WHAT THE BIBLE TEACHES:

Deuteronomy 24:5 An example of commitment expected.
I Peter 3:1-7 Wives and husbands committed to each other.
I Corinthians 7:4 Giving ourselves to each other.

EXPLORING OUR FEELINGS:

1. How do you feel about a 50-50 arrangement in marriage? Since few couples can ever reach a 100 percent commitment, should we then be satisfied with a good 50-50 agreement?

2. Someone has compared marriage to a business in which the husband is the president and his wife is vice-president. Would you like that arrangement in your home? Does this conform to the idea that the husband is the head of the wife as mentioned in Ephesians 5?

18

3. Does a personal commitment to Christ imply that our marriage problems are solved in that way? Do you feel that this keeps a marriage intact even when there are disagreements?

4. Margaret Meade, the noted anthropologist, suggests that it would be well for a couple to agree to live together in a sort of trial marriage for a year. There should be no children during that time. If this works out the marriage would be made permanent after the trial year. Would you take this suggestion seriously? Do you have a better solution? How can a couple gain a 100 percent commitment if they do not know how the marriage is going to work out?

5. In Deuteronomy 24:5 Israel was commanded not to send a husband to war during the first year of marriage. This was evidently to help the couple to establish a solid relationship. Does this suggestion have any value today?

6. Evaluate this statement: Each year a husband and wife live together in the bonds of marriage helps to strengthen the relationship, and makes the commitment stronger.

7. During which year in your marriage did you experience the greatest growth in your relationship, the first year, the tenth, or which one?

8. What does it mean that we accept each other "for better or for worse"? A man divorced his wife when she became mentally ill and was told that she would never be well again. Can you blame him for that?

3

FAMILY COMMUNICATIONS

A couple who sought marriage counseling faced a real problem in meaningful communication. The wife said that her husband was a good conversationalist at work. He also talked a good deal when they were at some social gathering or visiting with other people. But he did not talk a great deal at home. The husband then claimed that his wife was *always talking*, but never saying much. He was particularly irritated by her habit of talking to him while he wanted to listen to the six o'clock news. So they faced a real conflict in this area.

Communication Gaps

In many areas of life people are complaining about a breakdown in communications, or the "communication gap." This problem is increasing rather than decreasing. In the family, in society, in factories, in institutions, in schools, and in government, people do not understand each other; they do not hear what the other is really trying to say. In most of these areas, life would be more comfortable and pleasant if communications were improved. But when the barrier in communications is found in the family it can well destroy the home. Here is one place where there must be understanding of each other.

A couple who were in family therapy felt they had found a solution. Mary, the wife, had a few years of college and read a great deal. John, the husband, was a hard worker, but he never cared to read a book, or even a good magazine. He read his hunting and fishing magazines, and that was all. So Mary would point out an article to John, tell him to read it, and then they would have something to talk about. Somehow or other the solution failed, for you do not gain good relationships by discussing an article written by some professor or doctor. Communications must come from the heart, rather than from the pages of a book.

Using Questions

One of the secrets of improving communication is to learn the art of asking questions. It's hard to know what the other person is thinking about unless in one way or another you find out. Communication is not just sharing a bit of news or gossip, the word suggests that you "commune" with each other, that you find a common ground. Some people ask a lot of questions, just to gain information. The individual who is being bombarded with these questions answers No or Yes or Maybe, and as a result there is no real sharing or communing. There are some people (patients often feel that therapists are guilty of this) who always answer a question with a question. You don't communicate that way either.

A student described what went on in one of his college classes. The professor had asked whether there were any questions. This student ventured to ask one. Immediately the professor took him to task for asking such a dumb question and told him that if he had listened in class and read his textbook he would not come up with such nonsense. When a question is answered that way you can be sure not many more will be asked.

A question can be asked so that it shows genuine interest, but it can also become an inquisitorial one. When Billy comes home from school, Mother can ask, "What happened at school today?" She can ask the question in such a way that Billy is quite sure Mother had a call from the teacher that day. She can also ask it in a tone that shows she is

21

interested in him and wants to hear him talk about his day. If a mother asks this question very rarely, Billy will be suspicious when she does; as a result, he will tell no more than he must.

This questioning problem also applies to the husband-wife relationship. Hubby comes home a bit later than usual and is asked, "Where have you been all this time?" This question may be one of suspicion, or anger, but it can also be an expression of genuine concern. If it's suspicion or anger, it is not going to lead to very good communication. If it's concern it may lead to sharing experiences or feelings.

The Art of Listening

In our age we do not do a good job of listening. The whites have not really been listening to what the blacks have been saying. The more affluent ones have never really heard the true meaning of the words of the poor. We often close our ears, and yet we make profound statements about what must be done. Within the church also we are not really listening too well, for if we did we would realize that there is not so much of a conflict of ideas as many seem to think. We develop a large communications gap because we don't really understand what others are saying.

How then can we develop the art of listening to each other? It will demand of all of us a greater respect for those who need our help and acceptance. The old idea that children should be seen and not heard is false. It's good to give our children a chance to express themselves, and as mature parents we should be listening to the feelings that lie back of their words.

If we don't face up to the feelings of our fellow family members, soon the feelings will no longer be expressed, or we become phony even in our feelings.

A child comes home from school, he throws down his books and papers, and he says to Mother, "I hate my teacher!" Fortunately some mothers are understanding, but there are too many who will say, "You may not say that; you should love your teacher." This means that Mother is not really listening to her child, she is closing off the conversation, and in this way she will not really learn to know why her child hates the teacher on that particular day.

A daughter comes in a half-hour late from her date. Father gives her a good lecture about her dating habits, and the dangers of being out late. When she tries to explain what happened he interrupts with, "There is no excuse for coming in late, that is all there is to it." He hasn't been willing to listen to his daughter, and most likely she didn't hear what he said because of this.

Listening for Feelings

But listening to each other means more than just hearing the words people say. It means that we listen to the way things are said, to the emotional tone that is used, to the number of emotionally charged words; we listen to the feelings of people. There are cries for help that come to many of us, and if we are not skilled in the art of listening, we never quite perceive the real situation. In this desire to be heard is the call for love, for someone who cares and understands.

One of the best means of growth we have comes through marriage. On the other hand, a marriage can also stifle growth. There are roadblocks in the path of emotional and spiritual growth when there is a power struggle, or a good deal of jealousy in the relationship. But the finest and most pleasant way to grow is through conversation with our husbands or wives. This is one of the real purposes of marriage; we should seek for the enhancement of the personality of our mates, help them where they are weak and encourage them to become ever stronger in their good qualities. It seems like such a small thing, but just to talk things over together helps us greatly.

The Same Wavelength

Good communication means that we not only get on the same wavelength emotionally, but also spritually. There have always been differences between husbands and wives in their attitudes toward the Christian faith. Wives have found a deepening of faith and commitment that their husbands do not share. Sometimes husbands have had spiritual experiences that their wives do not fully understand. There is need today for a spiritual sharing, not just of facts and doctrines, but also of the deep, honest feelings about the Christian experience. Many of the small groups in the churches have been a genuine help in this direction, since husbands and wives share together in them. Here, too, we need to find a sense of unity in Christ.

WHAT THE BIBLE TEACHES:

Ephesians 4:15, 29 Speaking the truth in love.
Colossians 4:6 Let your speech be with grace.
James 3:6-10 The tongue and its control.
Malachi 3:16, 17 God takes note of our conversation.

EXPLORING OUR FEELINGS:

1. What is wrong with a person who is a good conversationalist in his work, or in a social setting, but does not talk very much at home?

2. In some families the children seem to dominate the conversation at the dinner table. Does this mean that parents have gone too far with this idea of listening? How can you help children to learn to listen?

3. Do you feel women are more talkative than men? Why?

4. When you find that your adolescents do not listen to your nice little lectures to them, what can you do about it? Is there a better way of reaching them?

5. Formerly in Bible classes and catechism classes the teacher or minister did most of the talking. Today every class has to be a discussion class. How do you feel about this newer method of teaching? Do you personally get more out of a meeting when dialogue is used than if there is a lecture? Does it really make any difference? Would you like dialogue in the sermon in church?

6. Do you think parents should talk "baby-talk" with little children? Do you feel that you should learn the language teen-agers use? Should you use this language when you talk with them?

7. How do you feel about a person who monopolizes the conversation? How can you close off the conversation of the compulsive talker without offending? Share your technique with the members of the class.

8. What can we do to improve communication and conversation in our homes? How do you handle the TV set when it conflicts with conversation?

9. Why is it more difficult to talk with the members of your own family about spiritual things than to talk with strangers about them?

4

QUALITIES OF A GOOD FAMILY LIFE

Many people seem to feel that marriage just happens to be good or bad, depending on how compatible the parties in marriage are. If they are in love all problems should solve themselves immediately, but if love fades there is little that can be done about it.

A good marriage, however, doesn't just happen; there are two people who are working at it, trying to make it a success.

Consideration

The apostle Peter gives some very good advice in this direction when he tells us in the third chapter of his first letter, "Husbands, live considerately with your wives, bestowing honor on the woman as the weaker sex, since you are joint heirs of the grace of life, that your prayers may not be hindered." I like that statement of Peter. He knew what he was talking about since he was also a married man. He tells us that if there is to be a good marriage there must be consideration.

Consideration means that we have a thoughtful and sympathetic regard and respect for others. It takes into account the circumstances and the feelings of others. The behavior of others is considered in the light of another's background and experiences. Peter suggests that husbands must be considerate of their wives, and wives of their husbands. It also brings out a few thoughts that are important in marriage today. It brings out the fact that there are going to be differences and incompatibilities in every marriage, often differences that cannot be completely removed, so they must be treated with consideration. Adjustments must be made.

Adjusting to Each Other

Mates in marriage are brought to the altar from different backgrounds, different homes, two different sets of parents who do not look at life in the same way, and often with a different set of values. When these two people move into the close ties of wedded life it will require a good deal of adjustment. A young man isn't used to being tied down to the responsibilities of caring for a wife, and a girl is not always ready to settle down to the mundane tasks of homemaking. These qualities in newlyweds must be harmonized, and this will take time and patience.

When there are needs for adjustments in the area of sex, or in the way money is to be handled, or in the matter of religion, it will require much consideration of the one with whom we are going to live twenty-four hours of the day, seven days a week

Sick marriages develop when one of the marital partners comes with the demand that everything in the family is going to run along the same lines that were found in the parental home. When a young wife says, "This is the way things were done in our home, and this is the way I want it in my home too," there is the beginning of a sick and poor relationship. When two people enter into marriage, both must approach the plans for the family openly and considerately.

Strength and Tenderness

It has often been said that a woman wants to be "taken, and taken care of." She wants to feel that she has been chosen by a man, even though she has often done most of the choosing herself. She likes to be swept off her feet, for basically she wants a husband who treats her with strength and tenderness. This is always one of the basic qualities of a good marriage; few women enjoy being married to a weak and effeminate man.

I hear far more often the complaint that a husband is too weak and passive, than too overpowering and dominant. Most wives feel that they have their own ways of handling a dominant male. They have neat little tricks, which are passed on from mother to daughter, clever means of disarming even the strongest of men. But when a woman succeeds in controlling her husband she does not feel quite right about it; she likes to think of him as a strong person, one on whom she can lean.

A discussion between a husband and his wife included the following: "I'm sick and tired of making all the decisions; I want you as my husband to make at least some of them." He answered, "But when I do make a decision, you put up an argument." She said, "Sure I do, but that doesn't mean that I want to win the argument. I want you to be strong enough so that I can't always win." The husband shook his head, because he could not understand that kind of reasoning. She said, "I guess the human part in me wants to control you, but the feminine part of me wants a man who is strong enough to stand up to me. I would then feel much more secure."

Frustration

I am sure that every husband has felt thoroughly frustrated when his wife projects this attitude. But this is the strange struggle we often find in families and homes. Husbands also feel this way at times. They put up a good fight, argue their point with conviction and force, but do not always like to win the argument. Children have the same inner conflict. They will argue long and loud against some suggestion or command of their parents, raising quite a fuss, but they do not always like to win the argument. This would mean that their parents are weak and to be secure they need parents who are strong. They need to know that there is authority in their parents.

To build successful relationships in the home, we need both strength and tenderness. An understanding parent is not afraid to allow his youngsters to argue with him. The parent who says, "I'm telling you this, and I don't want to hear your arguments," is basically a weak person. He is afraid that he will lose control, or that he will lose the argument. The secure parent can accept the arguments and discussions of his children because he has both the tenderness to listen to what they have to say, and the strength to withstand the attacks of the younger generation.

We all make mistakes, but with patience and determination we can satisfy the needs of our wives or husbands, and give a sense of inner security to our children. Even in our own hearts we have that basic need, to feel that our mates are strong but also tender—that the love they show flows from strength and not from a passive weakness. Maturity requires this of all of us. We must be strong enough to face the battle bravely, but tender enough to bind the wounds of those who are wounded and lost.

A Balanced Approach

The problem of all parents is to achieve a good balance of the two. We can move too far in the direction of tenderness so that we become pushovers for our children or our wives. We can also be so determined to show strength that we become harsh. To blend the two together into a harmonious relationship of love and concern is not easy, but it is important.

God has a perfect blending of the two. We are

told that He who numbers the stars also heals the broken hearts. That speaks of strength and also tenderness. This is also illustrated when Moses compares the care of God with that of the eagle caring for its young. The strong beak and powerful claws give a sense of security to the young birds. There is no tenderness worth having that does not find its source in strength and power. There is no grace sufficient that does not flow from one who is powerful and just.

WHAT THE BIBLE TEACHES:

I Peter 3:7, 8 The Revised Standard Version says: "Likewise you husbands, live considerately with your wives. . . ."

I Corinthians 13:4-7 Some of the qualities of love.

Deuteronomy 32:11, 12 A marvelous picture of both the strength and the tenderness of God.

EXPLORING OUR FEELINGS:

1. Do you agree that wives prefer a husband who is strong in his role in the family? Does this agree with the Women's Lib Movement? Do you think this movement agrees with Peter when he calls the wife "the weaker vessel?" Do you feel the woman is really the weaker vessel?

2. Some husbands like a wife who is a strong person. If both of them are strong personalities, does this cause a conflict? Is this bad?

3. In an article entitled "Tenderness, a New Form of Fatherhood" it was stressed that it is no disgrace for a father to change diapers, to put the children to bed, or to wash dishes. How do you feel about this in your family?

4. Tenderness is not passivity. What is the difference?

5. A wife is very meticulous about her housekeeping, her husband prefers the "lived in look." Should the husband respect his wife's feelings? Should she respect his feelings? How?

6. Can consideration be carried too far?

7. Do you agree that children feel more secure in the home when the parents are strong and firm? Someone said that it "takes strong parents to be successfully permissive." Do you see how this can be carried out in your family?

8. The family of a young husband was accustomed to swimming and boating on Sunday, and watching football games on TV on Sunday. His wife came from a home where this was not allowed. Should they compromise when they marry, or how should they handle such differences?

9. Can you see yourself as the wife or husband who would say, "Sure, I argue with you, but that does not mean that I want to win the argument"? Does that really make sense?

10. What does God's example of being strong and yet tender mean to you?

5

TRUSTING EACH OTHER

A young wife once told me, "I love my husband very much; but I don't trust him." This, of course, is a contradiction; one of the main ingredients of love is trust. It is not possible to really love a person who we feel might not be reliable, especially when it comes to the more personal factors in a marriage. Trust means that we rely on the integrity, justice, and faithfulness of another person. It is in this way that we trust God; we feel that He will keep His word and fulfill His promises.

Lack of Trust

I have found that one of the basic weaknesses of many marriages today is the lack of trust. In a sense, we are taught that it is not wise to trust others; through being too trusting, we often get hurt. There has been a genuine breakdown of our reliance on some of our national leaders, for they have shown by their conduct that they are not worthy of our confidence in them. We are taught that it is not wise to trust the word of a used car salesman, men who service our cars, or repairmen who fix our TV sets. "Always read the fine print of a contract or insurance policy," we are told, for the unsubstantiated words of a person cannot be accepted for truth. There are many who are not honest, so we must beware. It is sad to live in a world like this. In the past people would often make a contract or agreement with only a handshake, but without trust this sort of agreement is impossible.

But there are still certain relationships in which trust is a requirement. The church doesn't deal with its members by means of written contracts; they simply expect that the commitments of the church will be carried out. It would be impossible to write a job description for a minister or a binding contract for the work of an elder. Christians often trust a church leader because he is a representative of the God of truth.

Trust in the Family

Trust must also be present in the family. When a husband feels that it is necessary for him to call his wife on the phone at unexpected hours of the day to check up on her, there is something radically wrong. By doing this, he implies that he cannot rely on her word. If a wife feels the need of going through the pockets of her husband's suits, or checking on his whereabouts, there is a very unwholesome spirit in the marriage. But you would be surprised at the number of persons who do these sorts of things.

How do you develop a sense of trust in your mate? According to the dictionary, trust is built through experiences which we have with others. We know that a person is reliable when he has shown himself to be worthy of trust. We know whether a man is a reliable workman when we observe him working and see the results of his work. So also in the family, we learn to trust our mates when we observe their reliability. A husband will learn to trust his wife's way of handling finances when he has observed that her system is effective.

Expecting Faithfulness

One of the most basic trusts which should always be present in a marriage, is the trust in the faithfulness of one's mate. No marriage can be healthy when one of the mates is always a bit suspicious of the other, wondering whether there is some infidelity on his or her part. I know that some persons are insanely jealous of their mates. Some husbands wouldn't dare to allow their wives to see them talking with other girls. Other husbands are even jealous when their wives come to see a counselor. Such lack of trust reveals either one of two things: first, there may have been a break in the relationship causing one mate to feel insecure; but more commonly, a husband who does not trust his wife is projecting his own feelings about himself—he may not be sure that he will be faithful to her.

I have often seen a lack of trust in marriages in which there were premarital sexual relations or a premarital pregnancy. Many mates in such marriages seem to feel that if their mate was willing to have sexual relations with his (her) future wife (husband), he (she) may also be ready to have sexual affairs with others. This is one of the tragic results of these premarital affairs. Young people today often claim that such affairs are not wrong; but they do not realize that such activities leave a scar in the relationship—one that time does not necessarily heal.

Trusting Our Children

Parents also need to trust their children. A child learns the sense of trust in the family, so parents need to give their children an opportunity to show that they can be trusted. A mother who sends her junior high son to the grocery store with money can teach him to be trustworthy. Parents must also learn to trust their teen-agers in a dating situation. If we have laid a good moral foundation, have done our best to give some education in the basic facts of sex, we must learn to trust them. A suspicious parent can make a child rebel. A child may well say, "If my parents expect me to get into trouble, I might as well do it."

Mutual trust is a necessity in family living. Each

34

member of the family should learn to trust the other members. It's easy to say this, but it is very difficult to do. For we are human and we fail—we are not always trustworthy. But when we are truly committed to a good family life, we will know that we all learn from our failures; the way we handle the failures will also help others to trust us.

Basic to all of this is the trust we have in ourselves. When we solve the inner conflicts in the presence of a God whom we can trust implicitly, we will grow also in our reliability in family living. When this is mutual, when the family bows in the presence of God, when we are ready to confess our unreliability in each other's presence, we can learn the Christian art of trusting each other. We want to love and be loved. We also want to trust and be trusted and trustworthy.

WHAT THE BIBLE TEACHES:

II Samuel 6:16, 20-23 Michal shows that she did not trust David.

Genesis 27:5-13 A lack of trustful relations between Rebekah and Isaac.

Psalm 15:1-4 The qualities of a good man, worthy of trust.

EXPLORING OUR FEELINGS:

1. A husband became involved in a shady business deal. When his wife heard of it she was deeply shocked, for she was such a "trusting soul." Can people be too trusting? Are there times when a wife should not trust her husband, or a husband should not trust his wife? Can there still be a good marriage if there is a lack of trust?

2. A young husband regularly picked up his secretary on the way to work, since she lived in the same community. What do you think of that?

3. When you have a baby sitter take care of the children, who should drive her home, the husband or the wife? Does your answer betray a lack of trust, or are you possibly too trusting?

35

4. I have known of marriages where the wife did not know how much money her husband made. What are your reactions to this? Does this show a lack of trust?

5. Some games that are played at social gatherings require rather close bodily contact between men and women. Do you consider such contacts dangerous if your husband, or wife, is involved?

6. How do you know you can trust your teen-age boys and girls when they are out on dates? If you do not trust them, what does this reveal about your own dating practices?

7. There was some change lying on the TV set. Only you and one of your children are in the house. The money is gone and you suspect that your child has taken it. How do you handle this situation?

8. "A person who does not trust others cannot be trusted." Is this true? How does this apply to the family?

6

LOVE ALSO INCLUDES GRACE

All of life is an education in the art of loving. The little baby first learns to love his mother and his father, his brothers and sisters, aunts and uncles, and then in a wider circle, he must learn to love others. We go through certain stages in learning to love; at first it is our family, then our pals. We have sweethearts and then husbands or wives and children. It is a constant cycle. Grandparents love their grandchildren in a different way than they love their own children. At times, friends of long standing are closer than brothers and sisters.

Love also means different things to different people. For some, physical attraction is strong, and much of love has a sexual content. For others, it is a love for kindred souls with whom they like to discuss, or even argue. For some, it is the aesthetic side of life that unites together. But the basic love must be that of one person for another; not for what they have, or what they can offer, but for what they are. This is the love that lasts.

Paul, in I Corinthians 13, mentions various qualities of love. He views it like a prism that reflects various colors and hues, depending on the way the light strikes it at the moment. One of the qualities of love mentioned in several ways by Paul—one that is often forgotten—is that of grace—the willingness to forgive, or to overlook the failings and failures of others. This is not stressed a great deal. Often mates will speak of their partners with the words, "But I don't love him anymore, especially not after he treated me so badly."

In Case of Infidelity

Last week, in one afternoon, I counseled two

wives who had experienced the unfaithfulness of their husbands. Both of the husbands had been sexually involved with other women. One of them said that she could forgive him and take him back, for she felt that he had fallen into sin in a moment of weakness. The other was equally strong in stating that she could not forgive her husband and she was ready to divorce him. She even quoted the passage of Scripture which states that divorce is permissible in cases of adultery. What is the difference between these two? One had a love that was mixed with grace; the other felt that her husband had broken the relationship and as a result she could no longer love him.

What should a husband or wife do when there has been unfaithfulness: fight it out or get a divorce or separation? Much depends on the level of intimacy between the two partners in marriage. A great deal will also depend on the strength of the relationship between the two. Some marriages are able to weather the storm of infidelity, for there is an underlying relationship between the two that is not easily broken. Some unions are very fragile and even a severe difference of opinion sends the couple in opposite directions. There is no simple answer to infidelity.

Divorce?

The Bible does consider adultery to be a legitimate ground for divorce. This may be the answer when only a husband and wife are involved, but when children are included in the family, it would seem far wiser to try to lead a couple to forgiveness and a complete resolution of the differences between them. This is especially true since usually the "faithful partner" has contributed to the unfaithfulness of the other. Usually the girls who are willing to "go out" with a married man give him a listening ear when he tells how his wife does not really understand him, or is unwilling to satisfy his needs. This is often a "line" they use, but it has a lot of truth in it. Wives tend to take their husbands for granted.

One of the most difficult things for the spouse of an unfaithful mate is maintaining his self-image. If a husband chooses another woman as his companion, his wife will feel that he must think this woman is superior to her. The same thing applies to a husband with an unfaithful wife. Basically, it *is* a form of rejection. For a man is only *really* faithful to his own wife when he is wholly committed to her.

Should I Tell?

When someone asks me the question, "Should I tell?" I try to find out first how strong the marriage is, and whether it can actually weather that kind of storm. If a person who has sinned is confident that the "affair" is completely broken off, if the person feels that she is again right with God, if she is again building a sound and intimate relationship with her husband, then the problem will resolve itself—sometimes by means of a confession to her husband, sometimes not. There is no rule that applies in every case.

Divorce is to be avoided, if at all possible. It is only a last resort. Forgiveness, acceptance, and a lack of vindictiveness is always the Christian principle. All of us must say "except for the grace of God I would be that person." If we are really honest with ourselves, we all must say that.

The Real Test of Love

The real test of love does not come when everything runs along smoothly, but rather when there are problems. It's not so hard to love our children when they are well-behaved ladies and gentlemen.

But there are times when they are regular stinkers; then love is not so easy. But if there is no grace, they will be living in constant fear of making an error. We live in the same relationship with our loving Father in heaven. He sets before us the ideal, "Be ye perfect." But at the same time, He takes account of the fact that we are not going to be perfect, so He promises grace and forgiveness when we falter and sin. Then we do not live in constant fear lest we sin, but with the freedom that we enjoy since we have become "new creatures in Christ."

I believe that if there was more grace in our hearts, and in our homes, we would not be so afraid to come home in the evening and say, "I made a mess of it again." We'd know that we would find understanding there. A child could then freely come home and say, "I got a rotten mark on my paper," rather than hide the paper so that his parents will not see it. We would all find it easier to confess our faults to each other.

But since there is not much grace in the human heart, we try to hide our faults, we build up a neat front, we smile when we feel like crying, we deny that we have done anything wrong, and we end up hating ourselves for it. Marriage could be so much more wonderful and helpful if we could be open about our faults as we now are about our successes. This is a good way to test your family life: Are we really able to accept each other's failings and mistakes, so that we can be free to express them?

WHAT THE BIBLE TEACHES:

Leviticus 20:10 In the Old Testament the adulterer and the adulteress were both to be executed.
Matthew 19:9-12 Jesus speaks about adultery.
Matthew 18:21, 22 Jesus tells us how often we should forgive.

40

EXPLORING YOUR FEELINGS:

1. If a husband is unfaithful to his wife and becomes sexually involved with another woman, do you feel that a wife can really forgive? Can she forget? If she can't forgive would it be better to separate?

2. Today's teaching is that "affairs" in a marriage are just part of our liberated culture. How has this attitude influenced you? Do you think you are as shocked about sexual sins as your mother was? Is this progress?

3. If a husband, or wife, has been sexually involved with another person, should they always confess to their mates? Should they tell of moral indiscretions before marriage, or is it better to keep this a secret from their mates?

4. If your child has done something wrong and needs a spanking, should you first tell him that you forgive him, or should he first be spanked? Are there times when parents should tell their children that they cannot forgive them?

5. People who have sinned will often say, "God has forgiven me, why is it so hard for people to forgive me?" How would you answer this question? Do you think it is true?

6. If a husband is unfaithful to his wife, is it true, as it is so often said, that his wife has contributed to his sin? Is there ever an innocent party in a divorce?

7. Usually today when there has been unfaithfulness in marriage it is suggested that people go to a marriage counselor. How do you feel about this? Should the pastor be the marriage counselor?

8. Why is it so important in a family to show grace as well as love? Would your family survive without the spirit of forgiveness among its members?

7

LOVE AND ANGER

We all feel a bit ashamed of our anger and do all
we can to repress it. Most of us have been brought
up to believe "little boys (girls) don't get angry."
Possibly we have even been told that anger is
sinful—that if we become angry, we are bad. There
is even the strange and impossible statement made
by some child specialist telling parents never to
spank their children in anger; everybody knows,
however, that the parent won't spank unless he *is*
angry. Anger can and must be used in a creative
way.

Creative Anger

A young married woman was telling me that she
regretted that her parents never got angry at her, no
matter what she did. She said, "I wish my parents
had gotten mad at me for some of the things I did as
a kid; then I would have known that they cared
about me." Wives often feel that way about their
husbands. "He never gets angry with me, no matter what I do." Such a wife will begin to feel that her
husband is very unconcerned about her
behavior—he doesn't even care enough to get
angry. We often convince ourselves that by being
continually even-tempered with our spouses or our
children, we are doing them a favor. But I'm convinced that if we can't say, "I am awfully mad at
you," we have no business saying, "I really love
you." For love and anger go together.

Remember that beautiful incident in the life of
our Lord. First he berates the Pharisees in strong
terms. He calls them blind leaders, serpents, fools,
and hypocrites. But then follows that passage in

which Jesus pours out His loving heart in concern over Jerusalem! "How often would I have gathered thy children together as a hen gathereth her chickens under her wings but ye would not!" This shows how close together anger and love were in the heart of Jesus.

So must it be in our lives. We know that our anger is never sinless like that of Jesus. There is always so much of self in our anger. But there is also concern and love for others. We must not confuse anger with hatred. Hatred is the opposite of love, but anger can often be an expression of love. It certainly opens the doors for a deeper love. This becomes obvious after a good quarrel; when the anger has been resolved, the love is richer and deeper—now the two feel free to love.

Fear of Our Anger

One of the reasons why many conceal their anger is that they are afraid of what they will do or say when angry. Each individual has his own way of expressing anger—a way he has learned in earlier days of life. Some people cry when they are angry, but this is a poor expression; other people will not easily detect the feelings that lie behind our tears. Others go into periods of silence; this response, too, is hard to interpret. It is far better to be direct with our anger. Many persons will say, "You make me angry." This puts the blame on the other person. I find it much more effective to say, "I am getting angry with you." Then the expression of anger is direct, it tells what goes on in my heart. Honest directness in anger always pays.

It is always important to recognize our anger. Often husbands and wives refuse to admit their anger, saying instead that they are hurt or frustrated. These are just words that tell about anger in a different way. Anger often arises when we have

43

been hurt by what another person is saying or doing. We become angry when our attempts to accomplish something are blocked by another person—we are frustrated. Even a little baby gets angry when you hold him down tightly. If he could talk, he might say that he is frustrated, but since he can't talk he will just let out a good, loud, angry cry. In that way he is more honest than many adults.

Admitting Anger

It is often difficult in either group or individual therapy to make a person aware of his anger. All of us like to deny that we are angry, especially in the presence of others. It is also more difficult to admit our anger to some people than to others. A man will often deny that he is angry with his wife, but he has no trouble admitting that his children make him angry. Or a man will not admit to his anger toward his boss in the office, but he has no trouble admitting to this anger when he reaches home. Under some situations our anger is more threatening; for example, if you really told your boss what you thought about him at a given time, you might be looking for another job the next day. This is also true when there is a poor relationship between a husband and wife; they don't dare to admit anger for fear that their marriage will break up.

Love and Anger Go Together

Love and anger go hand in hand. But then we must be willing to express both. We would often like to wait. After all, tomorrow, when we have cooled down, we can admit how angry we were —but this does no good. We must deal with our anger immediately. Paul must have thought about this when he tells us that the sun must not go down on our anger. It's not good to let today's anger bother us tomorrow, because tomorrow will have enough occasions for anger again.

When love and anger are intermingled in our relationships, we will learn to express both of them freely and without resentment; then anger can become a healing power in a relationship that is in danger of breaking up.

Healthy Anger

There is such a thing as creative anger; we must learn to use it, for it frees our hearts so that other emotions can also flow freely. If anger is used to bully others, if it is a means to threaten others, if it becomes a personal attack on another individual, it will never be creative. This is not because the anger itself is wrong, but the way we use our anger is wrong.

Healthy anger can be a creative experience in the lives of people who live together, who meet each other in a church, or who argue over the backyard fence. This is one way we can fulfill in a measure the mandate, "Be ye angry and sin not."

WHAT THE BIBLE TEACHES:

Proverbs 15:1; 16:32 Controlled anger.
Matthew 5:22 The danger of anger.
Ephesians 4:26 Don't allow your anger to rule you.

EXPLORING OUR FEELINGS:

1. Some say that anger is always sinful. In view of the Bible passages given, is anger always wrong? Is there room for healthy anger?

2. When one of our children does something wrong, like breaking a nice vase, or spilling ink on the rug, do we have the right to be angry?

3. Why are many people afraid of their own anger? Should we try to curb the anger in our children by telling them that "nice boys and girls don't get angry"? How do you deal with temper tantrums in your youngsters? How about temper tantrums in your mates?

4. It has been said that if you don't dare to tell your mate

that you are angry with him you do not really love him. Why do we become angry with those we love more easily than with those we do not know too well?

5. What are some of the dangers of pent-up anger? How long can you remain angry with your mate or your children? Some people seem to be able to remain angry for several days or weeks so that they do not talk with each other. What's wrong with this?

6. A man said, "I never get angry with my wife, I love her too much for that." Would you like to be married to a person like that? Do you believe that some people never get angry in that way?

7. Have you found situations in your family where anger really helped to build better relationships? Share one of these experiences with the class.

8. In the book "The Intimate Enemy" by Bach and Wyden, it is suggested that when you have an argument, even an angry one, you should look for a solution in which both can win. Do you feel this is possible? Who usually wins the arguments in your family?

9. A father argued with his daughter and she finally said, "I suppose you are right, you're always right and I'm always wrong. That's the way it always is around here." Who won the argument? What is wrong with this kind of argument?

8

THE JOY CHILDREN BRING

This morning we received word that a new grandson had been born in our family. This is the eighth grandchild, and yet there is a thrill and excitement that fills the day. Each new child is a bundle of life, of opportunities and potentials. When you hold a baby in your arms, no matter how small and red-faced he is, you think of the possibilities and challenges into which this budding life arrives. You wonder what the future holds.

Why Have Children?

The only true motivation for having children is love and a desire to share and perpetuate that love. It takes a lot of loving to have a baby and bring him up to adulthood. Hopefully, each child is the result of that creative love on the part of parents—a symbol of a desire to give something to life. To take care of a helpless baby, to give him food when he cries, to console him when he is unhappy, to satisfy his need for love and affection to such an extent that he will fall asleep in your arms and feel secure—this is the joy that children bring to parents.

Having a baby is not entirely unselfish; parents get a satisfaction out of creating a new life. They like to see their own image reflected in the life of one who still has a long way to go. I think we feel this even more as grandparents. We know that our own years may well be limited in contrast to the young and tender age of the child we hold. We may believe that many years lie ahead of him and this thought gives joy.

We well know also the price of that love given to

children. When we minister to one who has just lost a little child through illness or accident, we see the heart-rending pain that love can cause when the love relationship must be broken. We see often the wounded love of parents who have loved deeply and then found their love answered by rebellion. We see other parent-child relationships broken by tragedy in a young person's life. Love always has a price that we must pay; pain is one of the costs of love.

The little baby becomes a greater source of joy when he can respond in a loving way to his parents. Often, he has opportunity to show the kind of love you have shown to him. He tries to comfort you when you are unhappy. He puts on his little act because he knows that this is something you enjoy.

Through the Eyes of a Child

One of the best things children can do for their parents or grandparents is to help them see the world through the eyes of a child. Though their span of interest is very small and they are flighty in their moods, they see little things in life with a sense of newfound wonder and awe. The squirrels robbing our bird feeders, the ducks at the duckpond, the new fallen snow, or the forbidden flowers that little hands pluck—they all show us the world through the eyes of a child. We often see things through the eyes of our prejudices, our bad experiences, and our failures; life can be grim. But children teach us the joy of the ordinary things and the beauty of things that seem drab to us.

Watching a child grow up in your own image can also be humbling and fascinating. He is a personality within himself, yet also an extension of the ego of his parents. It can be humbling to see your own hostility and anger in the temper tantrums of a little boy. Somehow, our own sins and imperfections look a little blacker when we see that we have passed them on to the next generation. But some of the good qualities also shine through.

Birth Control

I do feel that it is important to stress that it is not the quantity of children, but the quality, that really counts. Some parents are well able to have a family of eight, while others should limit themselves to two or three. It all depends on the situation. No one in the state or the community or the church should tell people how many children they can have, for this must be left to the conscience of the parents concerned.

The important thing is that we think in terms of the health of the family, both the parents and the children. There are some mothers who go through some form of emotional breakdown every time they have a baby. Some need repeated hospitalization either before delivery, or after. Some mothers have severe physical problems with child-bearing. Such factors can well be determining when plans are made for the size of the family.

Others have serious financial problems, and an added mouth to feed will complicate the situation even more. There can also be personal reasons for limiting the number of pregnancies. Sanctified common sense may dictate in these matters. Naturally, if parents limit their families only because of personal convenience, or the fact that they can live in greater affluence and comfort if they have only one or two children, this cannot be approved. The Christian conscience would rebel against such attitudes. It would mean that we are not fulfilling the God-given purpose of marriage.

In each case there must be a careful and prayerful consideration how we can best fulfill our role in life as a Christian. This must be a matter of the individual conscience of the parents.

Unwanted Children

We live in an age when many are looking for a

49

variety of cures for unwanted pregnancies, when parents are free to confess that one or more of their youngsters was an "unwanted child." When many children, and later on adults, suffer from this lack of love, it is important to stress the joy of children. All of us live by the pleasure-pain principle. We seek the things that give pleasure, and we try to avoid the things that give pain. The fact that children are born each day indicates that there must be pleasure in having children.

It should also be true for us that we not only look for the joy, but also face the responsibility. Love and acceptance do not mean pampering our children. They mean instead that we seek what is for their best—their highest good. And here there is another thing we can see in children: faith—the gentle trust in a loving Father. I often long for the simple faith that is expressed in the prayers of our grandchildren. Little things we do not consider to be worthy of prayer come into their focus, and they bring them to God.

One of the most marvelous gifts of a bountiful Creator is the desire to propagate ourselves, to join two hearts in the creative act of giving life to a child, and then to help to mold that life so that the image of God may be reflected there. This cannot solve the mystery of human birth; but it does help us to see the purposes of God realized through us, and through His marvelous love.

It's Tough to Be a Parent

It's tough to be a parent. But God has never promised that it would be easy to have children. There are many comments in Scripture about parents and children. This indicates that there has always been a problem between the generations. But the problems are not too big to handle if we accept them in a mature way, and if we truly believe in the covenantal promises of a loving God.

In the family we are not just dealing with a number of mouths to be fed, or feet that need shoes, but individuals with hearts and minds and souls. We bear the responsibility for these youngsters, for their spiritual and emotional and physical care and development. This would be an overwhelming responsibility if we felt that we must do this alone. Some of the most wonderful promises of God's gracious assistance have been given. It's up to us to accept the promises in humble faith.

WHAT THE BIBLE TEACHES:

Genesis 30:1, 2 The strong desire for children.
Matthew 19:13, 14 Jesus takes children into His arms.
Psalm 127:3-5 Children are a heritage of Jehovah.

EXPLORING OUR FEELINGS:

1. Since there does seem to be some danger of over-population in the next half-century, is it the Christian's duty to limit the size of his family? Should you feel guilty if you have eight children today? I feel that today people often look with suspicion at a family that has ten children. How do you feel about that?

2. A young couple said that since this was such a wicked world they did not think that it would be right to bring children into it. What would you say to them?

3. An obstetrician told a mother that she really should have an abortion, since he felt that having a full term child would endanger her physical and mental health. Would you have an abortion if this happened to you?

4. An ever-growing number of people today limit the number of children they bring into the world and then adopt a few children, especially unwanted "bi-racial children" or children with handicaps. What risks and problems will such people face? Should they take that risk? Would you be able to do this?

5. When people have a number of children, rather closely spaced, the father and especially the mother

lose much of their freedom. Children can then be a source of worry or they can hamper much social, or even church life. Do you feel that this robs people of feeling the "joy of having children"? Can parents really love all these youngsters, or will they love some more and others less? Can we really love each child equally well?

6. Were you brought up in a large family, or a small family? What difference does it make in individual growth if you were a member of a tribe, or an only child?

7. What is the healthy Christian attitude of parents to their children? How can we achieve that attitude? Mention a few hazards that prevent us from having this attitude.

9

SETTING LIMITS IN THE FAMILY

Whenever people live together, or work together, they need guidelines to prescribe limits for behavior. Only with such limits is healthy interaction possible. In a school, a factory, or an institution there must be some "dos" and "don'ts" that set limits for all who live or work there. Even a college dormitory must have guidelines. In the family, the parents are responsible for setting these guidelines and limits, and they must see to it that such rules are enforced.

Too many limits will make an institution out of a home, but too few limits will turn a home into bedlam. When we were tiny children, we needed limits for safety, for sharing, for hurting others, and for respecting the feelings of others; and we still need these limits. But when a family sets such guidelines, they must make sure that they are fair, consistent, firm, and definite. The limits should apply to every member of the family living at home.

Often parents get disgusted when their children ignore the limits. A father might say: "How often do I have to tell you to behave?" or, "When are you going to learn that you can't do this?" And when children are young, they need someone to set and enforce these limits for them—they need external controls. (As a child grows up, he develops internal controls.) Children have their ups and downs, even more than adults do; at times they act like little angels, but at other times their sinful natures seem to take over.

Enforce the Limits

It is not easy to teach a child to remain within the limits—somewhere between "You must" and "You may not." A child will take all the liberties his parents will allow. That is why the limits must be set by mutual consent so that parents work with each other, and not at cross purposes. Children have to be taught. A mother had been teaching her three-year-old to share with other children. So the child was sharing a toy with another boy. Suddenly he got up and went to another three-year-old, grabbed a little truck out of his hand, and said, "Let's share." He seemed to feel that sharing meant he could take as well as give. He needed further instruction in the meaning of sharing.

Playing Parents Against Each Other

Often when parents set limits, the children will play one parent over against another. A teen-ager asked her mother whether she could use the car for some errand. When her request was refused, she waited for a little while and asked her dad the same question. He said, "I guess you can if you're careful." This was a case where one member of the parental team was played over against the other. The junior or senior high youngsters know how to get their way, and often allow a conflict to develop between parents. When limits are set, they must be consistently applied. This requires good communication between parents.

It may be well to set limits also among the parents of playmates in a given community. When our children play with others, it is good that there be consistent limits for the whole group. The mothers in one neighborhood decided to make a rule that their children, who played together, might not cross the street. One day this little gang went to one mother and asked for permission to cross the street;

she refused. They tried another; she also refused. Finally they told one of the mothers that their parents wouldn't mind if they crossed the street if she would give the approval. So she did, and soon the telephone was ringing; the neighbors wanted to know why she gave approval while the others had refused. But often, when these cute little rascals use their clever tactics, they make one parent feel like a mean person if she does not consent. Children are very clever at manipulating people with their cute smiles and pleading voices.

Parental Limits

To have children live within limits may require parents to live within limits also. In fact, all of us have limits set on us. We may only drive our cars at safe speeds. We have limits as to how much we eat, especially when we are on a diet. We may also need to set limits on ourselves for the sake of the children. When you tell children that they may not watch a TV show since it is only for adults, it is better if you don't watch it either, especially if it's on prime time. If your children see you breaking the law by speeding, or running a red light, you can't say a great deal when they are caught cheating or stealing. Parents must live within the same kind of limits that they set for their children. Our liberty is curbed by the fact that we may not offend one of these little ones, or cause them to stumble.

Setting limits is essential if there is to be authority in the family. A growing youngster wants limits; he needs limits to give him a sense of security. When these limits have been clearly spelled out, he will know what he may, or may not, do. The permissive parent thinks he is doing his child a favor by not setting limits. He often punishes a child by whim. The little boy who was spanked because he tore his pants said, "Out there in the ball park everybody cheered me, and I was a real hero when I slid into home base; but when I get home I get spanked for it." In the home we need to be consistent. It is very unsettling for a youngster when one day his dad laughs at something he does, and the next day he gets spanked for the same thing.

We are living in times of unprecedented opportunities for children and young people—for all of us. But the great danger of these opportunities and advantages is that people become spoiled by their own prosperity. Giving a child his way—letting him determine his own desires and needs, is not necessarily an expression of love. Smothering a child with love is actually a form of rejection. Love requires controls, and controls require discipline.

God's Example for Us

We could take an example from the way God deals with His children whom He loves very dearly. He gives out of the abundance of His love the bountiful gifts of life, even more than we need. But He does not spare His children from the testing experiences that are so important for their spiritual growth. Paul speaks of contentment in that marvelous chapter in Philippians, but then he says that he has *learned* to be abased and he has *learned* to abound. He was unbroken by adversity, unspoiled by prosperity. This is the kind of thing that leads to a strong and contented personality.

God sets limits for all of us. There are the great commands He gives which determine the things we may not do, and the things we must do. Between the extremes of these two is the realm of human choice, the liberty we have as Christians. Some make that great area of life rather broad; others make it rather narrow. But when God sets His limits for us, and for our children, who are we to question Him?

WHAT THE BIBLE TEACHES:

Hebrews 12:6-11 Human discipline and God's discipline.
Proverbs 13:24 Sparing the rod.
I Samuel 2:22-25 Eli takes a rather permissive attitude towards his sons' actions.
I Timothy 4:12 Being an example.

EXPLORING OUR FEELINGS:

1. There have always been spoiled children. Do you think there are more of them today than in a previous age? Give some reasons for your answer.

2. The number of teen-agers in institutions is constantly on the increase. Do you feel that the parents of such adolescents are worse, or different, than the rest of us?

3. Dr. Dobson makes the remark, "Some of the little terrors who are unmanageable in the classroom are mistakenly diagnosed as having emotional problems." Do you agree with this remark?

4. How do you react to parents who draw up a written set of guidelines for behavior for the family? Would you like to have such guidelines on your family bulletin board?

5. What do you do when you notice that your child is playing one parent over against the other? For example, when they want the use of the family car. Would you say that dad is the head of the house, he should decide; would you talk it over together; or would you talk it over together in the presence of the child?

6. Parents had taught their children not to cross the street when the light was against them. A little boy was walking with his father, and although the light was red he walked across the street with his boy. The little boy called this to his attention. The father said "When you are alone you may not go against the light, but when I am with you it is perfectly safe," How do you react to this?

7. Do you feel that parents set too many limits for their children? Too few limits? Too many unenforceable limits?

8. If Christ has set us free, why does He still set limits, such as in I Corinthians 8:9-13?

10

THE AUTHORITARIAN PARENT

Two labels are often used to describe the position of parents in the home. One is an authoritarian relationship, the other a permissive relationship. The use of such labels still tells us very little about the relationship, for there are varying degrees of authority and permissiveness. Parents may also be authoritarian in one area of life, while they are rather permissive in another.

Authority—Authoritarian

We often find that people confuse the terms "authoritarian" and "authority." It's a bit hard to find a good distinction between them. As I see it, the "authoritarian" approach is that of a dictator who takes a totalitarian view of life. You must obey a dictator or you are in danger of losing your life. You obey him, no matter how unjust his demands may be, for he embodies all authority within himself.

Authority is necessary to experience the good life, and this is true also in the home. But the authority expressed in the home grows out of love and concern. Its purpose is to promote the well-being of the members of the family, not just to assert the right to rule. When our purpose is merely to assert our right to rule, we are being authoritarian, and authoritarianism leads to rebellion and the attempt to circumvent commands. We all know youngsters who are brought up in authoritarian homes where the word of father or mother is law. Such youngsters may not ask why, they may not talk back, they must simply obey because the parents have said so. Youngsters who grow up in such homes become adolescents who feel the need to rebel.

I have often noticed among young people in the church that those who come from stern and rigid families cause a good deal of trouble in Bible school or Sunday school classes. It seems as if they have to let loose when they are away from the watchful eyes of their parents. They are often the ones who feel the need to rebel, to show their anger toward their parents by rejecting the things the parents have tried to teach them. It's little wonder that this is so, for they have learned only the obedience of fear, not the obedience that grows out of love.

Authority in Love

The authoritarian approach is not the Scriptural one. In the Bible, parents are encouraged to deal with their children, and others, in love. They are not to provoke their children to anger, but to bring them up in the fear of the Lord. Parents must exercise authority, but this authority is vested in parents by God. It must grow out of mutual respect for each other's rights, but also out of a common loyalty to the One in whom all authority is vested.

It's not that I would like to swing to the opposite extreme of complete permissiveness. Parents sometimes use this as the easy way out. They don't want to inhibit the growing personalities of their little darlings, and so they let them grow up like Topsy. The danger of the overly permissive approach is that children do not learn to respect authority. If children do not learn a sense of authority in the home, they will not learn it anywhere else. The child will not learn to respect teachers if he does not respect parents. He will have little regard for the rights and property of others if he does not have his fingers slapped at home when he reaches out to that which he should not touch.

There is, then, the fact that parents must assert authority, but they should not be authoritarian. They should exercise the privilege and responsibility given to them to nurture the child in an atmosphere that is rich in Christian love and acceptance. This means that they will not allow the child to do as he pleases, but they will teach the child to obey, to respect his parents and to honor them. This is not the authority of the big stick, but the authority of love. It's not a matter of fear, but respect. And parents can only expect the respect of their children when they earn it by a warm and loving relationship.

Respect Must Be Earned

I am deeply convinced that to gain the respect of our children we must earn it. The man who frequently gets drunk, and in his drunken stupor abuses his wife and children, will say, "I have no right to expect the esteem of my wife and children." He has not earned their respect. But this is equally true of the father who loses his temper, and in his tantrums beats his children or breaks furniture. A father who is arrested for leaving the scene of an accident loses the respect of his teen-age boys.

Parents who make use of sarcasm and hostile ridicule also lose the respect of their children. Name calling, deriding expressions, and demeaning comparisons usually lead to resentfulness. A father who said to his son, "If you had more between your ears than a jackass, you would know how to take care of yourself," is not helping gain his son's respect. It is not that children have to be pampered, but rather treated fairly and in love. We must respect our children, if we want them to respect us.

A child may be beaten into submission when he

is young, he may need to be spanked because this is the only language he really understands. But when boys or girls pass their tenth birthday the value of spanking is no longer a factor. They may be forced to do something against their will, but they will still be of the same bent of mind. It's only when there is love and respect that a child can learn self-control, so that he will do what is right out of proper inner motivations.

Spiritual Qualities

There is possibly a greater danger with the authoritarian approach. I know that a number of people have a religion of fear. They think of God as a God of anger, as a bully whom they must obey because He is stronger than they are. They do not have a concept of a loving Father, for they have always felt that authority means anger and rejection. The child's concept of the heavenly Father is often patterned after his concept of their earthly father.

Paul stresses that we "should not provoke our children to anger." Peter tells us that members of the family should treat each other with consideration. But plain common sense teaches us that we must treat fellow members of the family as human beings, with feelings and emotions that are constantly developing. The family, then, cannot be seen as a dictatorship, ruled by the iron hand of a stern father. It is composed of thinking, reasoning, feeling, and trusting individuals, bound together with ties of a common love for the God who gives life, and for each other, with human needs and hungers that can only be satisfied in an atmosphere of mutual respect.

Authority is vital to the home—authority vested by God in the parents. But this authority should be a living expression of love.

61

Here the Christian faith offers a tremendous power. We do not serve God because we are afraid of Him, or because this is the thing to do, but because we can say with Paul, "The love of Christ overmasters me." This is the mightiest dynamic for Christian living; it has moved away from fear to love, from the negative to the positive, and from selfishness to seeking to do His will. This is the purpose of discipline. It is the purpose of discipline in the home and of God's discipline for the forming of a Christian man and woman.

WHAT THE BIBLE TEACHES:

Ephesians 6:1-3 God requires obedience of children to parents.

Ephesians 6:4 Parents should not provoke children to anger.

I John 4:7, 8 A powerful incentive for loving each other.

Colossians 3:20 Children should obey and parents should not discourage them.

EXPLORING YOUR FEELINGS:

1. When you think of your own parental home, were your parents authoritarian, or were they permissive? How did this influence your personality? How does it reflect itself in your dealings with your children?

2. It has been said that excessive emphasis on authority and also excessive permissiveness are both indications of the rejection of a child. A mother says, "I love my child so much, I would never think of spanking him." What is your reaction?

3. We are told that parents who spank their youngsters should never use an instrument, only their hand. It has also been said that we should never spank when we are angry. Do you feel that you should comply with these suggestions?

4. How do you react to the father who says that he gave his son such a severe spanking "that he will never forget it"? Can you remember the spankings you received when you were young?

5. Should a child respect his parents just because they

are his parents, or should the parents earn that respect? Can you force a child to respect his parents?

6. A mother said that she would far prefer to reinforce her son when he does something good, than to punish him for something bad. But she said "he never does anything that I can reward him for." What's wrong in this situation?

7. Find some guidelines to distinguish between "asserting authority" and being "authoritarian."

8. Is God "authoritarian" in His approach to His people?

11

THE LITTLE IRRITATIONS

Even the families that are basically sound and healthy will have misunderstandings. Most of these differences are not caused by major problems, but by minor irritations. And if we do not handle them in adult ways, these little irritations can often become bigger problems. The regular and daily routine of living together will lead to situations in which we get on each other's nerves. We are often impatient with the traits of behavior that make no sense to us.

The Bathroom

One of the aspects of family living that causes considerable irritation is the use of the bathroom. Some newer homes may have a number of bathrooms so that the family does not have to make use of common facilities, but in most families this little room can be a source of conflict. When brother Ted leaves a ring in the bathtub or the wash basin, sister Sue may find it distasteful to have to first remove the debris left by him before she can use them. A number of towels may be left lying around in disarray, or the bathroom may be used as a place to dry part of the family wash.

When we bring up the subject of irritating things in groups of couples, one of the things often mentioned is the way one or two of the members use the tube of toothpaste. Some get angry when their spouse does not replace the cap. Even more commonly there is irritation when one of the members squeezes the tube from the middle, especially when Father feels that the only way to treat a tube is to squeeze it carefully from the bottom.

Clothing

Clothing in the family can also be a source of irritation. Children and teen-agers will often leave their clothing lying around in conspicuous places after they have finally selected the wardrobe they feel to be suitable for the day. Girls as well as boys can have their room in a terrible state of disarray. Mothers often think that they have failed in giving the proper training when they view such a scene. This is often a source of conflict. Where husband and wife must share the same closet, you have the same kind of conflict. Good habits would demand neatness and orderliness, but on the other hand, such irritations should not be allowed to become a major source of conflict in the family.

The Telephone

The use of the telephone is another source of irritation. One member of the family may sometimes misuse this instrument by long conversations so that no one else can use it, or so that no one can get through to the home. This can be most exasperating to members of the family, and at times can create some real crises. Some families have tried to regulate this by setting rules and time limits on the use of the phone. This can be unreasonable also, for a considerable amount of the social life of a teen-ager centers around the telephone. It may be necessary to set up some compromise as to its use.

The Way People Talk

Another source of irritation is the way people talk to each other in the family. Parents often resent that young people "tell it like it is." They would prefer that there be a little restraint and less forthrightness. Children often feel that parents are preaching, or they are talking like "old fogies." Here too it is important to be considerate of each other. I recently had contacts with a family where the use of "You" or "Thou" in prayer was a matter of irritation. The parents did not like to use "You"; the children did not like "Thou." The compromise was made that parents and children take turns in their table prayers, and each makes use of the pronoun which is most comfortable for him. It's a small matter, but it can lead to a lot of heat and anger.

Family Chores

A constant battle is carried on in some families about who is supposed to do what around the house. The modern home is a marvel of modern conveniences, and many of the menial tasks which we once had to do are no longer a part of everyday living. But there are still enough routine tasks that must be done, and that leads to conflict. Bringing out the garbage, hanging out the clothes, and bringing in firewood are largely events of the past. But the waste basket must still be emptied, the lawn must be mowed, and dishes must be washed or put into a dishwasher. There are many chores that modern ingenuity has not been able to conquer.

It is good that it is so. Children must learn that they are a part of the family. They must learn that as members of that family they have responsibilities for the work that must be done around the home. This often creates conflict. Many parents find that battling with their children about housework is hardly worthwhile. It is much easier to do it themselves. This, however, is not an ideal home life. People are supposed to be living on the same level, and there is no reason why one or two should be living like slaves.

Set an Example

But there are other things involved. Parents must first of all set an example in their own attitude toward the household chores. A boy of ten will hate to empty the waste baskets, just as much as his dad does. Washing the car can be just as much drudgery for a boy as it is for his dad. It seems wrong for parents to ask their children to do the kind of work they do not like to do themselves. I noticed a father in our community mowing the lawn with a nice, shiny, self-propelled mower, while his teen-age son had to trim the edges and sweep off the sidewalk. I am sure the boy would have been much happier if he had had the mower, and his dad had had the broom.

Some parents use household chores as a form of discipline or punishment. This gives a child false ideas about work. It implies that work is a curse —something no one likes to do. Work should be faced as a responsibility we have, which we can enjoy, and which forms part of living. If you see the unhappiness of a man who is out of work, or who can't work because of an illness, you soon learn to appreciate the joy of being able to work.

The home must train youngsters to face responsibilities. The problem in many homes is that children are pampered. They feel that they should never have to lift a finger to share in the work. Such youngsters grow up with the feeling that someone else will do the work for them, and that they can ride through life without ever soiling their delicate hands.

Removing Irritations

Why do people irritate each other in the home? I do not believe that we often go out of our way to irritate other members of the family. It is not a deliberate act, but it grows out of the close relationship between members of the family. And it is very rare that you can say that the one person is wrong and the other is right, for when there are irritations, usually two are at fault. So it will require a lot of give and take on the part of all parties concerned. I do think that it is good to express our feelings. It is not good to keep them bottled up. But feelings must also be expressed with a certain amount of restraint.

We cannot avoid daily irritations. It is part of living. But we can learn to live with irritations in a reasonable and Christian way. The person who cannot face irritations is acting like a spoiled child; the mature person expects that life's road is not always going to be smooth and even.

The finest way to handle frustrations is to look at them in the spirit of love and forgiveness. Family living requires a measure of grace. We must give the other members the right to make mistakes, for we know we also make ours. Then we should be ready to forgive others, even as God in Christ forgave us.

WHAT THE BIBLE TEACHES:

Song of Solomon 2:15 The little foxes that spoil the vineyard.

Matthew 23:21-24 The Pharisees straining at a gnat.

Matthew 6:25-32 Worrying about less important things.

EXPLORING OUR FEELINGS:

1. When teen-age boys, or girls, refuse to keep their bedroom neat, what should parents do? Should mother clean the bathroom when the youngsters mess it up?

2. Do you think a family should have rules as to how long, or how often a member may use the phone? Should such rules also apply to parents? How do you solve the telephone conflict in your home?

3. In some families there is a real conflict about the kind of music that is listened to. Some parents try to prevent their children from listening to rock and roll. How do you think this should be handled?

4. How do you handle the conflicts about TV? Dad would like to watch a football game, but the children would like to see their programs. Who wins?

5. Why do little irritations cause so many problems in the family, when there are many important things that need to be resolved? Is this an indication of a lack of love in the home? Does this indicate that we are too small in our character, or too narrow-minded?

6. Teen-agers like to dress and groom their hair like the rest of the youngsters at school. If you refuse to allow them their choices they will stand out from the rest of the crowd. Should parents then insist on conventional hair-cuts and loose-fitting sweaters? Is this something that is important enough to you to create a conflict of the generations?

7. The Bible stresses that little things are important, such as little sins, white lies, or "idle words." May we as Christians overlook the little things so that we only deal with big issues?

8. How do you feel about using the family chores as a form of punishment?

12

SHARING FINANCIAL RESPONSIBILITY

Mark Twain made a New Year's resolution pledging: "This year I will live within my income, even if I must borrow money to do it." The financial responsibility of many people is not much better than that. Although people often talk about their debts rather lightly, at least one of the two partners in a marriage spends sleepless nights worrying about family expenses.

Many have real problems in family financing. In today's world it is very easy to have a billfold that contains a dozen credit cards. Few questions are asked when you submit a credit card; but then the statement is sent, and soon the second notice arrives which adds a high rate of interest. The bill keeps on growing each month until payment is made. There are no easy payment plans.

The Family Treasurer

The treasurer of the family has a lot of power and often uses it in the family power struggle. I still meet a wife every now and then who doesn't know the exact amount of her husband's paycheck. She is given an allowance, and is expected to live within it; she is not aware of how much her husband uses. It is his money and he can use it as he pleases. Of course, this arrangement shows a lack of trust in family relations. In an increasing number of homes, the wife takes the responsibility for finances. She too can use this as a weapon in the family power struggle—the hand that holds the purse string rules the family. If a married couple feels the need to engage in a power struggle, money is an effective means. Some people live constantly in the shadow of a dollar. Money has often been called "home-maker or home-breaker No. 1." Financial conflict is one of the primary causes of America's unprecedented divorce rate. In one study 48 percent of people who had marital problems attributed it to the almighty dollar.

Financial Difficulties

Sometimes financial difficulty results from health problems in the family. A child with a chronic illness can drain all financial reserves and leave a load of debt. An illness or accident can cause the income to be greatly reduced. Sudden layoffs in factories can cut off all source of regular income. Such situations, over which we have no control, can happen in any home. In many homes they become a cause of conflict instead of the experience for growth which they could be.

But money, or the lack of it, is often a cause for worry, and it leads to a lot of anxiety. Finance is also one of the primary conflicts within the family. When this becomes a god, people have not found a good foundation for living. The most common worry of people is about the material things of life. Poverty is no virtue, neither is wealth. It all depends on the attitude we take, for money can hide the face of God.

A Sense of Values

The ability to bring up a family with a good sense of values does not depend on how large our house is, or how one's standing is on the stock market. There are other factors that are far more imporant. I have known children from very wealthy families who were well-mannered and who had developed beautiful characters. At the same time there are children, raised in poverty, who have developed a high sense of values, and who live a happy and productive life. It all depends on where we, as parents, have placed our emphasis.

They say in our land that "every man has his price." This is true. But the price is not in terms of dollars and cents, or whether we "have" or "have not." It depends on the inner resources of the soul and mind. Agur prayed for neither riches nor poverty (Prov. 30:8). He preferred a happy medium. Wealth can be a blessing if we see that everything we have and are comes from God. Poverty need not be a disgrace, if we learn the spirit of being content in whatever state we find ourselves. We must learn to be unspoiled by prosperity and unbroken by adversity. This develops Christian character both for us and for our children.

Using Our Money

Today's Christian family faces some real choices in the distribution of their money. A number of families face the decision of whether to send their children to a Christian or a state college. The high costs of tuition can take a large part of a family's income. Such choices should be carefully and critically made. Some are making these choices rather lightly today.

Responsible financing also involves giving for the church and various kingdom causes. It is easy to say that we can't afford to pay our share of the costs for the church and its institutions. But basic in the management of money is developing a sense of maturity in its use. To use it as a source of power is childish and ridiculous. To make it a source of family conflict is also immature. This is also true when couples speak of "my money" and "your money." The mature approach requires the trusting attitude of a joint account and the use of the phrase "our money." In this partnership, the responsibility should include the children as well as the parents. If it is hard to meet expenses, it's good to let the children know that they are also expected to live on an austerity budget. When children earn their own money, they too should share in the responsibilities of the family.

Partnership with God

Possibly the best way to deal with this problem is to take God into this partnership. It will be easier to give our share to God and to others if we recognize that He is also a shareholder in the financial partnership of the family. There would be a lot less quarreling about money if we did this.

WHAT THE BIBLE TEACHES:

I Timothy 6:10 The love of money, the root of evil.
James 5:1-6 The danger of riches.
Malachi 3:7-10 God's command about tithing.
II Thessalonians 4:10-12 The need to work with our own hands.

EXPLORING OUR FEELINGS:

1. Why do married couples argue a great deal about money? Do you agree that the family treasurer has considerable power to control the family? Who should handle the finances?

2. When a wife works and has her own source of income, how can you avoid the matter of "my money," "your money," and "our money?" A joint account causes a good deal of conflict at times.

3. A mature person is neither spendthrift nor miser. Mention some ways in which our use of money reflects immaturity. Suggest some mature ways of dealing with finances.

4. Parents should teach their children to handle finances. How can we go about this, especially when there is not a great deal of money in the family?

5. Is it a good thing to punish a child by taking away his weekly allowance? Should you reward a child with

money when he does something extra for the family, or gets good grades in school?

6. Do you feel that the law of tithing still is in effect in the New Testament church? How strict should we be about this? What should we include in the tithe? Can you include the tuition of your daughter if she attends a Christian college?

7. If we give the Lord one-tenth of our income, may we then use the other nine-tenths as we please? Does God lay down any rules for the spending of money?

8. If you can well afford it, may you indulge in luxuries? Our parents seldom went to a good restaurant, today this is common. Is it right to spend money along this line? A man built a home that cost $100,000, drove a very expensive car, and had a good-sized cottage on the lake. Is this in line with the Christian attitude towards money? Are there any limits?

9. A man was asked to move to a distant city in line with his work. It shook up his family a great deal, the children moved away from friends and they had to search for another church home. Is a man justified to do this just for the sake of a promotion and a doubling of his income?

13

CHRISTIAN NURTURE IN THE HOME

One of the finest definitions of a Christian marriage is given by J. K. Morris in his book *Premarital Counseling.* "A Christian marriage is one involving a Christian man and woman each dedicated to his understanding of God's purpose for himself and his spouse, and their children, to achieve the measure of the fullness of the stature in Christ." He goes on, "In a marriage that is truly Christian both the husband and the wife will respect the developing personality of the other, aid its enhancement, strengthen it where it is weak and encourage it in its goodness."

One marriage form speaks of the "mutual enrichment of the lives of those entering this state." All of this implies that a good family relationship is one in which the members are interested in Christian nurture and development, not only of the children, but also of the husband and the wife. It implies a relationship in which growth is not only possible, but growth is encouraged.

Spiritual Differences

A great deal of inequity can also develop in families in the spiritual qualities that husband and wife possess. In former days we would often find that the father was more developed as far as his knowledge of the Bible and the doctrines was concerned. The father was supposed to be the priestly head of the house, and I remember with deep appreciation the knowledge and insight of some elders in the churches I served. The mother would often have to say, "I really don't know too much about that, you will have to ask my husband."

When there is a great difference in spiritual development between husband and wife, there are often conflicts. I have met some mothers who have had a deep spiritual experience, and who talk about this freely, while the husband feels uneasy about it all, and often criticizes or minimizes the things his wife confesses. I also know of situations where the opposite is true, where the husband is the one who talks about a vital faith in his own life. This means that husband and wife have not kept pace with each other; they have allowed the differences between them to increase. While their common faith in God should unite them, it tends instead to separate them.

We must be concerned about the developing personality of our mates. We should try to help them move toward the measure of the fullness of the stature in Christ. But to accomplish this, spiritual exercises should be shared, and each should try to help the other to grow. Only in this way can we set a pattern for our children.

The home is the basic instrument for the nurture also of our children. There is a real danger among us that we are content to leave this side of the training of our children to the school, or to the church. But the training in the church and the school may not be a substitute for the home; instead, they should complement the home. The home has the special task of adding spiritual warmth to the life of a child. Here the emotion can run freely: we can weep when our hearts are broken, but we can laugh with joy when we see the healing love of the Savior.

Teaching Spiritual Values

I am afraid that we often use the wrong approach to teaching such things as honesty, sincerity, clean living, and a proper concern for the needs of others.

A sense of right and wrong is not developed by merely telling our children that certain things are right and others are wrong. We need to impress on them that we all must live the kind of life that reflects the Christian spirit. We may not separate morality from religion, for morality without the upward look has little value. So when the family gets together around the dinner table, each member must confess that there have been sins and failures, that there are many things we should not have done, many that we ought to have done but failed to do. But there is the blessing of forgiveness through the work of Christ, and we all want to seek more and more to please Him.

All of this requires a simple faith in a loving and forgiving God. One of the fruits of that faith is a life that reflects that true forgiveness is found only when we have a firm determination to conquer the sins that remain in our lives. We cannot expect forgiveness if we plan to continue in the same sin anyway, at least we cannot feel forgiveness. This is the spirit we must communicate to our children and to each other.

A Place to Grow

I like to think of the family as a place where people can grow. Each member of the family must be allowed the room to grow. There is no finer place for spiritual, emotional, and experiential growth than the family. This is one of the reasons why God has established the home. If we do not develop in this way, we are missing the real purpose of family living. The whole covenantal concept is involved here.

The family altar fits into this pattern. This is the place where a Christian style of living is practiced and stressed. A lot of preaching is not demanded; instead parents must present an example of godliness in the pattern of living with ourselves, with each other, and with others outside of the family circle. Communication becomes a necessary tool in family living, for only in the measure that we truly communicate, by word *and* deed, will we accomplish the goal of the Christian family.

Honesty, purity, truthfulness, love, concern for others, and a deep desire to share the faith we have in Christ—these all must be taught. We are but tools in the hand of the Spirit of God to accomplish this. We have our children with us only a few impressionable years. We should use this time well.

Influence of the Home

The influence of the home is not that it is an educational institution like the school, but rather that faith here must be lived and shared. We can be ever so phony in church, but we can't get by with that in the home, for the close ties of husband and wife, of parents and children, will show up whether we are real or not. This may be evidenced in the prayers at the table, but it is evidenced far better in the way we talk about others, about the church, the way we talk to each other, and even more in the way we treat each other. The home has as its great purpose to encourage the developing personality of our mates, and of our youngsters.

There is nothing that can substitute for the home in Christian nurture.

WHAT THE BIBLE TEACHES:

Deuteronomy 6:4-9 The responsibility of parents to give spiritual nurture to children.
Proverbs 22:6 "Train up a child. . . ."
Psalm 78:4 We must tell our children.
Ephesians 6:4 Provoke not—but nurture them.

EXPLORING OUR FEELINGS:

1. How have you handled the recent evils in government in your family? Some have used it as a source of humor, others use it as a means to break down confidence in government. What is the Christian approach?

2. There are many things written and on TV that break down the moral consciousness of people. Should we keep our children from such influences, or should we help them to face up to them? How can we do this?

3. Some parents use religion to whip their children into line. What is the difference between using religion, being religious, and teaching religion? Give some examples.

4. Some young people say that they are "overfed" on religion. How do you answer that argument? Is it possible to get too much religion in our youth?

5. Do you feel that the family altar is a good way to teach the Christian faith? How do you do this? Is it good to read from a "children's Bible?"

6. Is it true that actions speak louder than words? It's rather common that Dad and Mother have an argument, or a fight. How should you handle this with the children? Should parents admit that they are wrong?

7. How do you try to teach such qualities as honesty, truthfulness, consideration, neatness, and reverence? How does the Christian faith enter into such teaching? Do you find lectures on such subjects effective?

8. You may have found some methods of Christian nurture that have been effective in your home. Share some of these with the rest of the group so that you help each other in this difficult area of family life.